P9-CRB-985

My Journal

on my way to a

NEW & BETTER

/ME/

Copyright © 2018 Happy Books Hub
All rights reserved.

For any inquiries or questions regarding our books, please contact us at: happybookshub@gmail.com

ISBN: 978-1985865181

week 1	1	2	3	4	5	6	7
week 2	8	9	10	11	12	13	14
week 3	15	16	17	18	19	20	21
week 4	22	23	24	25	26	27	28
week 5	29	30	31	32	33	34	35
week 6	36	37	38	39	40	41	42
week 7	43	44	45	46	47	48	49
week 8	50	51	52	53	54	55	56
week 9	57	58	59	60	61	62	63
week 10	64	65	66	67	68	69	70
week 11	71	72	73	74	75	76	77
week 12	78	79	80	81	82	83	84
week 13	85	86	87	88	89	90	

30 Days
to form a
NEW HABIT

Determine your new
DAILY GOALS & HABITS:

Cross a BIG X
over each day you
ACCOMPLISH
your new habit(s)

60 Days
to enjoy a
CHANGING YOU

Time to
CELEBRATE
your progress

90 Days
to welcome your
NEW ME

20 THINGS to start doing now

1. Keep a food journal. If you bite it write it.
2. Drink a lot of water and green tea.
3. Eat fruits and vegetables (more greens) + natural food.
4. Avoid processed food.
5. Go for a walk / bike ride.
6. Ditch the elevator for the stairs.
7. Dance, dance, dance it out!
8. Stretch daily to increase flexibility.
9. Go outside more.
10. Try yoga or meditation.
11. Go to bed earlier.
12. Wear clothes that make you happy.
13. Stop thinking negative thoughts about yourself or anyone else.
14. Do not judge yourself.
15. Do not compare yourself to others.
16. Throw away things you don't need.
17. Enjoy little things in life.
18. Next time you want to give up remember why you started.
19. Remember that all your efforts now will surely pay in the end.
20. Do it badly, do it slowly, do it inconsistently, do it any way you have to, but **do it anyway**. And then say hello to your NEW ME!

DAY 1 : My Starting Point

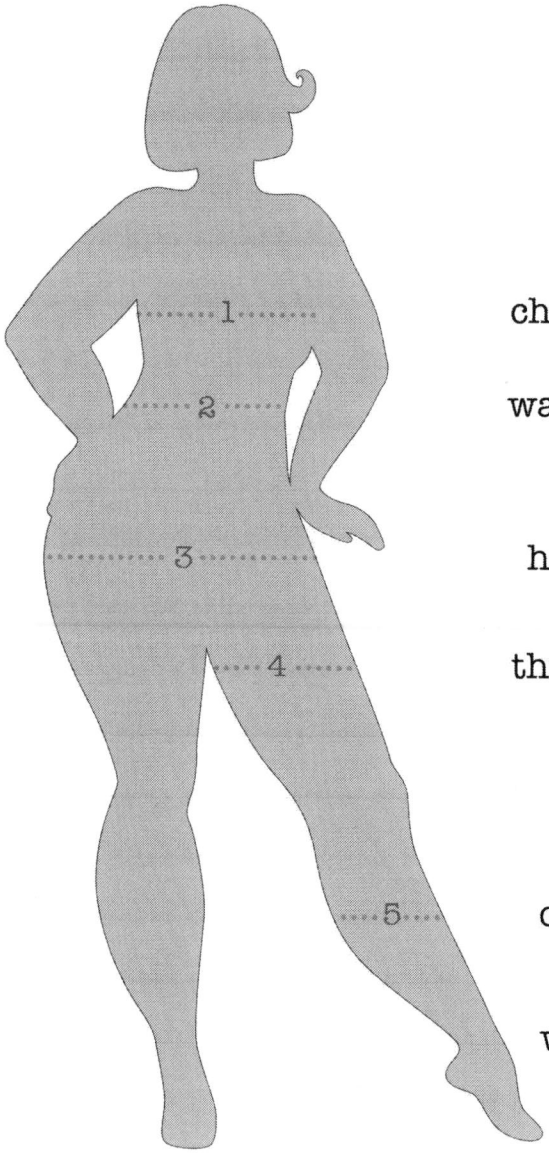

chest [1] .....

waist [2] .....

hips [3] .....

thigh [4] .....

calf [5] .....

weight .....

MY GOALS:

I am gorgeous the way I am! ... but here is what I'd like to improve: .....

.....

.....

.....

DAY 1

BREAKFAST

LUNCH

DINNER

SNACKS

WATER

SLEEP TIME

EXERCISE / ACTIVITY

How I feel today about my food & exercise

CRAVINGS / RESPONSE

Something to make tomorrow better:

DAY 2

BREAKFAST

LUNCH

DINNER

SNACKS

WATER

SLEEP TIME

EXERCISE / ACTIVITY

How I feel today about my food & exercise

CRAVINGS / RESPONSE

Something to make tomorrow better:

DAY 3

BREAKFAST

LUNCH

DINNER

SNACKS

WATER

SLEEP TIME

EXERCISE / ACTIVITY

How I feel today about my food & exercise

CRAVINGS / RESPONSE

Something to make tomorrow better:

DAY 4

BREAKFAST

LUNCH

DINNER

SNACKS

WATER

SLEEP TIME

EXERCISE / ACTIVITY

How I feel today about my food & exercise

CRAVINGS / RESPONSE

Something to make tomorrow better:

DAY 5

BREAKFAST

LUNCH

DINNER

SNACKS

WATER

SLEEP TIME

EXERCISE / ACTIVITY

How I feel today about my food & exercise

CRAVINGS / RESPONSE

Something to make tomorrow better:

DAY 6

BREAKFAST

LUNCH

DINNER

SNACKS

WATER

SLEEP TIME

EXERCISE / ACTIVITY

How I feel today about my food & exercise

CRAVINGS / RESPONSE

Something to make tomorrow better:

DAY 7

BREAKFAST

LUNCH

DINNER

SNACKS

WATER

SLEEP TIME

EXERCISE / ACTIVITY

How I feel today about my food & exercise

CRAVINGS / RESPONSE

Something to make tomorrow better:

DAY 8

BREAKFAST

LUNCH

DINNER

SNACKS

WATER

SLEEP TIME

EXERCISE / ACTIVITY

How I feel today about my food & exercise

CRAVINGS / RESPONSE

Something to make tomorrow better:

DAY 9

BREAKFAST

LUNCH

DINNER

SNACKS

WATER

SLEEP TIME

EXERCISE / ACTIVITY

How I feel today about my food & exercise

CRAVINGS / RESPONSE

Something to make tomorrow better:

DAY 10

BREAKFAST

LUNCH

DINNER

SNACKS

WATER

SLEEP TIME

EXERCISE / ACTIVITY

How I feel today about my food & exercise

CRAVINGS / RESPONSE

Something to make tomorrow better:

DAY 11

BREAKFAST

LUNCH

DINNER

SNACKS

WATER

SLEEP TIME

EXERCISE / ACTIVITY

How I feel today about my food & exercise

CRAVINGS / RESPONSE

Something to make tomorrow better:

DAY 12

BREAKFAST

LUNCH

DINNER

SNACKS

WATER

SLEEP TIME

EXERCISE / ACTIVITY

How I feel today about my food & exercise

CRAVINGS / RESPONSE

Something to make tomorrow better:

DAY 13

BREAKFAST

LUNCH

DINNER

SNACKS

WATER

SLEEP TIME

EXERCISE / ACTIVITY

How I feel today about my food & exercise

CRAVINGS / RESPONSE

Something to make tomorrow better:

DAY 14

BREAKFAST

LUNCH

DINNER

SNACKS

WATER

SLEEP TIME

EXERCISE / ACTIVITY

How I feel today about my food & exercise

CRAVINGS / RESPONSE

Something to make tomorrow better:

DAY 15

BREAKFAST

LUNCH

DINNER

SNACKS

WATER

SLEEP TIME

EXERCISE / ACTIVITY

How I feel today about my food & exercise

CRAVINGS / RESPONSE

Something to make tomorrow better:

DAY 16

BREAKFAST

LUNCH

DINNER

SNACKS

WATER

SLEEP TIME

EXERCISE / ACTIVITY

How I feel today about my food & exercise

CRAVINGS / RESPONSE

Something to make tomorrow better:

DAY 17

BREAKFAST

LUNCH

DINNER

SNACKS

WATER

SLEEP TIME

EXERCISE / ACTIVITY

How I feel today about my food & exercise

CRAVINGS / RESPONSE

Something to make tomorrow better:

DAY 18

BREAKFAST

LUNCH

DINNER

SNACKS

WATER

SLEEP TIME

EXERCISE / ACTIVITY

How I feel today about my food & exercise

CRAVINGS / RESPONSE

Something to make tomorrow better:

DAY 19

BREAKFAST

LUNCH

DINNER

SNACKS

WATER

SLEEP TIME

EXERCISE / ACTIVITY

How I feel today about my food & exercise

CRAVINGS / RESPONSE

Something to make tomorrow better:

DAY 20

BREAKFAST

LUNCH

DINNER

SNACKS

WATER

SLEEP TIME

EXERCISE / ACTIVITY

How I feel today about my food & exercise

CRAVINGS / RESPONSE

Something to make tomorrow better:

DAY 21

BREAKFAST

LUNCH

DINNER

SNACKS

WATER

SLEEP TIME

EXERCISE / ACTIVITY

How I feel today about my food & exercise

CRAVINGS / RESPONSE

Something to make tomorrow better:

DAY 22

BREAKFAST

LUNCH

DINNER

SNACKS

WATER

SLEEP TIME

EXERCISE / ACTIVITY

How I feel today about my food & exercise

CRAVINGS / RESPONSE

Something to make tomorrow better:

DAY 23

BREAKFAST

LUNCH

DINNER

SNACKS

WATER

SLEEP TIME

EXERCISE / ACTIVITY

How I feel today about my food & exercise

CRAVINGS / RESPONSE

Something to make tomorrow better:

DAY 24

BREAKFAST

LUNCH

DINNER

SNACKS

WATER

SLEEP TIME

EXERCISE / ACTIVITY

How I feel today about my food & exercise

CRAVINGS / RESPONSE

Something to make tomorrow better:

DAY 25

BREAKFAST

LUNCH

DINNER

SNACKS

WATER

SLEEP TIME

EXERCISE / ACTIVITY

How I feel today about my food & exercise

CRAVINGS / RESPONSE

Something to make tomorrow better:

DAY 26

BREAKFAST

LUNCH

DINNER

SNACKS

WATER

SLEEP TIME

EXERCISE / ACTIVITY

How I feel today about my food & exercise

CRAVINGS / RESPONSE

Something to make tomorrow better:

DAY 27

BREAKFAST

LUNCH

DINNER

SNACKS

WATER

SLEEP TIME

EXERCISE / ACTIVITY

How I feel today about my food & exercise

CRAVINGS / RESPONSE

Something to make tomorrow better:

DAY 28

BREAKFAST

LUNCH

DINNER

SNACKS

WATER

SLEEP TIME

EXERCISE / ACTIVITY

How I feel today about my food & exercise

CRAVINGS / RESPONSE

Something to make tomorrow better:

DAY 29

BREAKFAST

LUNCH

DINNER

SNACKS

WATER

SLEEP TIME

EXERCISE / ACTIVITY

How I feel today about my food & exercise

CRAVINGS / RESPONSE

Something to make tomorrow better:

DAY 30

BREAKFAST

LUNCH

DINNER

SNACKS

WATER

SLEEP TIME

EXERCISE / ACTIVITY

How I feel today about my food & exercise

CRAVINGS / RESPONSE

Something to make tomorrow better:

DAY 31

BREAKFAST

LUNCH

DINNER

SNACKS

WATER

SLEEP TIME

EXERCISE / ACTIVITY

How I feel today about my food & exercise

CRAVINGS / RESPONSE

Something to make tomorrow better:

DAY 32

BREAKFAST

LUNCH

DINNER

SNACKS

WATER

SLEEP TIME

EXERCISE / ACTIVITY

How I feel today about my food & exercise

CRAVINGS / RESPONSE

Something to make tomorrow better:

DAY 33

BREAKFAST

LUNCH

DINNER

SNACKS

WATER

SLEEP TIME

EXERCISE / ACTIVITY

How I feel today about my food & exercise

CRAVINGS / RESPONSE

Something to make tomorrow better:

DAY 34

BREAKFAST

LUNCH

DINNER

SNACKS

WATER

SLEEP TIME

EXERCISE / ACTIVITY

How I feel today about my food & exercise

CRAVINGS / RESPONSE

Something to make tomorrow better:

DAY 35

BREAKFAST

LUNCH

DINNER

SNACKS

WATER

SLEEP TIME

EXERCISE / ACTIVITY

How I feel today about my food & exercise

CRAVINGS / RESPONSE

Something to make tomorrow better:

DAY 36

BREAKFAST

LUNCH

DINNER

SNACKS

WATER

SLEEP TIME

EXERCISE / ACTIVITY

How I feel today about my food & exercise

CRAVINGS / RESPONSE

Something to make tomorrow better:

DAY 37

BREAKFAST

LUNCH

DINNER

SNACKS

WATER

SLEEP TIME

EXERCISE / ACTIVITY

How I feel today about my food & exercise

CRAVINGS / RESPONSE

Something to make tomorrow better:

DAY 38

BREAKFAST

LUNCH

DINNER

SNACKS

WATER

SLEEP TIME

EXERCISE / ACTIVITY

How I feel today about my food & exercise

CRAVINGS / RESPONSE

Something to make tomorrow better:

DAY 39

BREAKFAST

LUNCH

DINNER

SNACKS

WATER

SLEEP TIME

EXERCISE / ACTIVITY

How I feel today about my food & exercise

CRAVINGS / RESPONSE

Something to make tomorrow better:

DAY 40

BREAKFAST

LUNCH

DINNER

SNACKS

WATER

SLEEP TIME

EXERCISE / ACTIVITY

How I feel today about my food & exercise

CRAVINGS / RESPONSE

Something to make tomorrow better:

DAY 41

BREAKFAST

LUNCH

DINNER

SNACKS

WATER

SLEEP TIME

EXERCISE / ACTIVITY

How I feel today about my food & exercise

CRAVINGS / RESPONSE

Something to make tomorrow better:

DAY 42

BREAKFAST

LUNCH

DINNER

SNACKS

WATER

SLEEP TIME

EXERCISE / ACTIVITY

How I feel today about my food & exercise

CRAVINGS / RESPONSE

Something to make tomorrow better:

DAY 43

BREAKFAST

LUNCH

DINNER

SNACKS

WATER

SLEEP TIME

EXERCISE / ACTIVITY

How I feel today about my food & exercise

CRAVINGS / RESPONSE

Something to make tomorrow better:

DAY 44

BREAKFAST

LUNCH

DINNER

SNACKS

WATER

SLEEP TIME

EXERCISE / ACTIVITY

How I feel today about my food & exercise

CRAVINGS / RESPONSE

Something to make tomorrow better:

DAY 45

BREAKFAST

LUNCH

DINNER

SNACKS

WATER

SLEEP TIME

EXERCISE / ACTIVITY

How I feel today about my food & exercise

CRAVINGS / RESPONSE

Something to make tomorrow better:

DAY 46

BREAKFAST

LUNCH

DINNER

SNACKS

WATER

SLEEP TIME

EXERCISE / ACTIVITY

How I feel today about my food & exercise

CRAVINGS / RESPONSE

Something to make tomorrow better:

DAY 47

BREAKFAST

LUNCH

DINNER

SNACKS

WATER

SLEEP TIME

EXERCISE / ACTIVITY

How I feel today about my food & exercise

CRAVINGS / RESPONSE

Something to make tomorrow better:

DAY 48

BREAKFAST

LUNCH

DINNER

SNACKS

WATER

SLEEP TIME

EXERCISE / ACTIVITY

How I feel today about my food & exercise

CRAVINGS / RESPONSE

Something to make tomorrow better:

DAY 49

BREAKFAST

LUNCH

DINNER

SNACKS

WATER

SLEEP TIME

EXERCISE / ACTIVITY

How I feel today about my food & exercise

CRAVINGS / RESPONSE

Something to make tomorrow better:

DAY 50

BREAKFAST

LUNCH

DINNER

SNACKS

WATER

SLEEP TIME

EXERCISE / ACTIVITY

How I feel today about my food & exercise

CRAVINGS / RESPONSE

Something to make tomorrow better:

DAY 51

BREAKFAST

LUNCH

DINNER

SNACKS

WATER

SLEEP TIME

EXERCISE / ACTIVITY

How I feel today about my food & exercise

CRAVINGS / RESPONSE

Something to make tomorrow better:

DAY 52

BREAKFAST

LUNCH

DINNER

SNACKS

WATER

SLEEP TIME

EXERCISE / ACTIVITY

How I feel today about my food & exercise

CRAVINGS / RESPONSE

Something to make tomorrow better:

DAY 53

BREAKFAST

LUNCH

DINNER

SNACKS

WATER

SLEEP TIME

EXERCISE / ACTIVITY

How I feel today about my food & exercise

CRAVINGS / RESPONSE

Something to make tomorrow better:

DAY 54

BREAKFAST

LUNCH

DINNER

SNACKS

WATER

SLEEP TIME

EXERCISE / ACTIVITY

How I feel today about my food & exercise

CRAVINGS / RESPONSE

Something to make tomorrow better:

DAY 55

BREAKFAST

LUNCH

DINNER

SNACKS

WATER

SLEEP TIME

EXERCISE / ACTIVITY

How I feel today about my food & exercise

CRAVINGS / RESPONSE

Something to make tomorrow better:

DAY 56

BREAKFAST

LUNCH

DINNER

SNACKS

WATER

SLEEP TIME

EXERCISE / ACTIVITY

How I feel today about my food & exercise

CRAVINGS / RESPONSE

Something to make tomorrow better:

DAY 57

BREAKFAST

LUNCH

DINNER

SNACKS

WATER

SLEEP TIME

EXERCISE / ACTIVITY

How I feel today about my food & exercise

CRAVINGS / RESPONSE

Something to make tomorrow better:

DAY 58

BREAKFAST

LUNCH

DINNER

SNACKS

WATER

SLEEP TIME

EXERCISE / ACTIVITY

How I feel today about my food & exercise

CRAVINGS / RESPONSE

Something to make tomorrow better:

DAY 59

BREAKFAST

LUNCH

DINNER

SNACKS

WATER

SLEEP TIME

EXERCISE / ACTIVITY

How I feel today about my food & exercise

CRAVINGS / RESPONSE

Something to make tomorrow better:

DAY 60

BREAKFAST

LUNCH

DINNER

SNACKS

WATER

SLEEP TIME

EXERCISE / ACTIVITY

How I feel today about my food & exercise

CRAVINGS / RESPONSE

Something to make tomorrow better:

DAY 61

BREAKFAST

LUNCH

DINNER

SNACKS

WATER

SLEEP TIME

EXERCISE / ACTIVITY

How I feel today about my food & exercise

CRAVINGS / RESPONSE

Something to make tomorrow better:

DAY 62

BREAKFAST

LUNCH

DINNER

SNACKS

WATER

SLEEP TIME

EXERCISE / ACTIVITY

How I feel today about my food & exercise

CRAVINGS / RESPONSE

Something to make tomorrow better:

DAY 63

BREAKFAST

LUNCH

DINNER

SNACKS

WATER

SLEEP TIME

EXERCISE / ACTIVITY

How I feel today about my food & exercise

CRAVINGS / RESPONSE

Something to make tomorrow better:

DAY 64

BREAKFAST

LUNCH

DINNER

SNACKS

WATER

SLEEP TIME

EXERCISE / ACTIVITY

How I feel today about my food & exercise

CRAVINGS / RESPONSE

Something to make tomorrow better:

DAY 65

BREAKFAST

LUNCH

DINNER

SNACKS

WATER

SLEEP TIME

EXERCISE / ACTIVITY

How I feel today about my food & exercise

CRAVINGS / RESPONSE

Something to make tomorrow better:

DAY 66

BREAKFAST

LUNCH

DINNER

SNACKS

WATER

SLEEP TIME

EXERCISE / ACTIVITY

How I feel today about my food & exercise

CRAVINGS / RESPONSE

Something to make tomorrow better:

DAY 67

BREAKFAST

LUNCH

DINNER

SNACKS

WATER

SLEEP TIME

EXERCISE / ACTIVITY

How I feel today about my food & exercise

CRAVINGS / RESPONSE

Something to make tomorrow better:

DAY 68

BREAKFAST

LUNCH

DINNER

SNACKS

WATER

SLEEP TIME

EXERCISE / ACTIVITY

How I feel today about my food & exercise

CRAVINGS / RESPONSE

Something to make tomorrow better:

DAY 69

BREAKFAST

LUNCH

DINNER

SNACKS

WATER

SLEEP TIME

EXERCISE / ACTIVITY

How I feel today about my food & exercise

CRAVINGS / RESPONSE

Something to make tomorrow better:

DAY 70

BREAKFAST

LUNCH

DINNER

SNACKS

WATER

SLEEP TIME

EXERCISE / ACTIVITY

How I feel today about my food & exercise

CRAVINGS / RESPONSE

Something to make tomorrow better:

DAY 71

BREAKFAST

LUNCH

DINNER

SNACKS

WATER

SLEEP TIME

EXERCISE / ACTIVITY

How I feel today about my food & exercise

CRAVINGS / RESPONSE

Something to make tomorrow better:

DAY 72

BREAKFAST

LUNCH

DINNER

SNACKS

WATER

SLEEP TIME

EXERCISE / ACTIVITY

How I feel today about my food & exercise

CRAVINGS / RESPONSE

Something to make tomorrow better:

DAY 73

BREAKFAST

LUNCH

DINNER

SNACKS

WATER

SLEEP TIME

EXERCISE / ACTIVITY

How I feel today about my food & exercise

CRAVINGS / RESPONSE

Something to make tomorrow better:

DAY 74

BREAKFAST

LUNCH

DINNER

SNACKS

WATER

SLEEP TIME

EXERCISE / ACTIVITY

How I feel today about my food & exercise

CRAVINGS / RESPONSE

Something to make tomorrow better:

DAY 75

BREAKFAST

LUNCH

DINNER

SNACKS

WATER

SLEEP TIME

EXERCISE / ACTIVITY

How I feel today about my food & exercise

CRAVINGS / RESPONSE

Something to make tomorrow better:

DAY 76

BREAKFAST

LUNCH

DINNER

SNACKS

WATER

SLEEP TIME

EXERCISE / ACTIVITY

How I feel today about my food & exercise

CRAVINGS / RESPONSE

Something to make tomorrow better:

DAY 77

BREAKFAST

LUNCH

DINNER

SNACKS

WATER

SLEEP TIME

EXERCISE / ACTIVITY

How I feel today about my food & exercise

CRAVINGS / RESPONSE

Something to make tomorrow better:

DAY 78

BREAKFAST

LUNCH

DINNER

SNACKS

WATER

SLEEP TIME

EXERCISE / ACTIVITY

How I feel today about my food & exercise

CRAVINGS / RESPONSE

Something to make tomorrow better:

DAY 79

BREAKFAST

LUNCH

DINNER

SNACKS

WATER

SLEEP TIME

EXERCISE / ACTIVITY

How I feel today about my food & exercise

CRAVINGS / RESPONSE

Something to make tomorrow better:

DAY 80

BREAKFAST

LUNCH

DINNER

SNACKS

WATER

SLEEP TIME

EXERCISE / ACTIVITY

How I feel today about my food & exercise

CRAVINGS / RESPONSE

Something to make tomorrow better:

DAY 81

BREAKFAST

LUNCH

DINNER

SNACKS

WATER

SLEEP TIME

EXERCISE / ACTIVITY

How I feel today about my food & exercise

CRAVINGS / RESPONSE

Something to make tomorrow better:

DAY 82

BREAKFAST

LUNCH

DINNER

SNACKS

WATER

SLEEP TIME

EXERCISE / ACTIVITY

How I feel today about my food & exercise

CRAVINGS / RESPONSE

Something to make tomorrow better:

DAY 83

BREAKFAST

LUNCH

DINNER

SNACKS

WATER

SLEEP TIME

EXERCISE / ACTIVITY

How I feel today about my food & exercise

CRAVINGS / RESPONSE

Something to make tomorrow better:

DAY 84

BREAKFAST

LUNCH

DINNER

SNACKS

WATER

SLEEP TIME

EXERCISE / ACTIVITY

How I feel today about my food & exercise

CRAVINGS / RESPONSE

Something to make tomorrow better:

DAY 85

BREAKFAST

LUNCH

DINNER

SNACKS

WATER

SLEEP TIME

EXERCISE / ACTIVITY

How I feel today about my food & exercise

CRAVINGS / RESPONSE

Something to make tomorrow better:

DAY 86

BREAKFAST

LUNCH

DINNER

SNACKS

WATER

SLEEP TIME

EXERCISE / ACTIVITY

How I feel today about my food & exercise

CRAVINGS / RESPONSE

Something to make tomorrow better:

DAY 87

BREAKFAST

LUNCH

DINNER

SNACKS

WATER

SLEEP TIME

EXERCISE / ACTIVITY

How I feel today about my food & exercise

CRAVINGS / RESPONSE

Something to make tomorrow better:

DAY 88

BREAKFAST

LUNCH

DINNER

SNACKS

WATER

SLEEP TIME

EXERCISE / ACTIVITY

How I feel today about my food & exercise

CRAVINGS / RESPONSE

Something to make tomorrow better:

DAY 89

BREAKFAST

LUNCH

DINNER

SNACKS

WATER

SLEEP TIME

EXERCISE / ACTIVITY

How I feel today about my food & exercise

CRAVINGS / RESPONSE

Something to make tomorrow better:

DAY 90

BREAKFAST

LUNCH

DINNER

SNACKS

WATER

SLEEP TIME

EXERCISE / ACTIVITY

How I feel today about my food & exercise

CRAVINGS / RESPONSE

Something to make tomorrow better:

DAY 90 : Hello New Me!

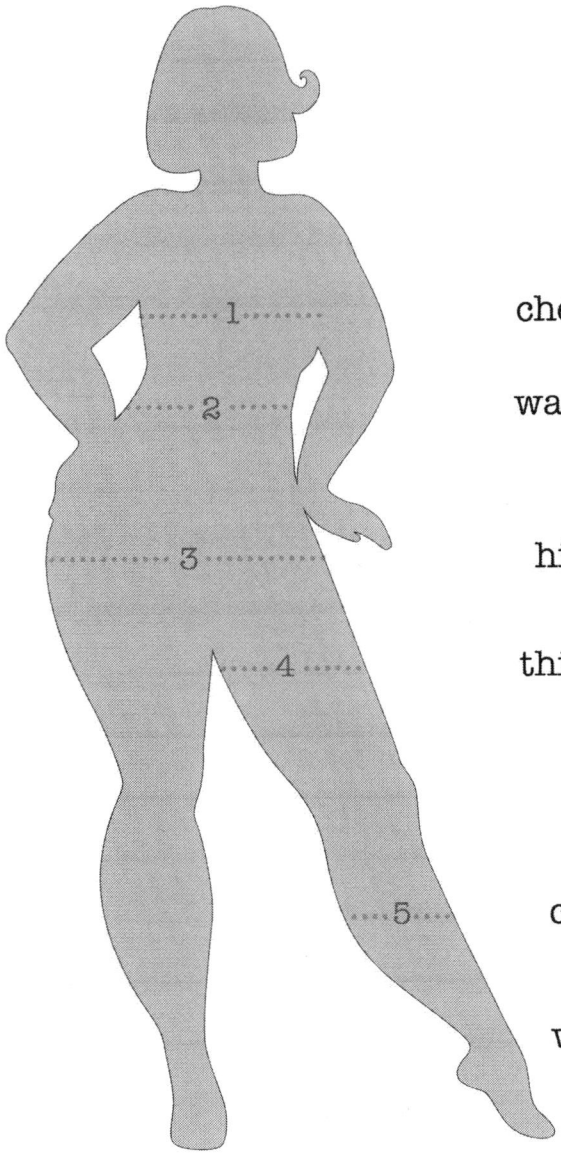

chest [1] .....

waist [2] .....

hips [3] .....

thigh [4] .....

calf [5] .....

weight .....

RESULTS:

I am still gorgeous! Habits to keep, things to improve: .....

.....

.....

.....

Hey, Gorgeous!

The book you have in your hands is brought to you by Happy Books Hub. We have a passion for creating books that can improve and add joy to people's lives. Hopefully this journal will accomplish just that for you!

If you have any suggestions on how to improve it, or what we can change or add to make it more useful particularly to you, please don't hesitate to contact us at **happybookshub@gmail.com**
We would be more than happy to consider how to apply your suggestion to this journal's next edition.

Thank you for buying Hello New Me journal!

Please, support us and leave a review!

Love,
Happy Books Hub